GEO

CIRCULATING WITH THE LISTED PROBLEM(S):

Pen Scribbles

RAD

1/20/09

Lexile: _____

AR/BL: 1.3

AR Points: 0.5

The Life Cycle of a

Cat

by Lisa Trumbauer

Consulting Editor: Gail Saunders-Smith, Ph.D.

Consultant: Ronald L. Rutowski, Professor,
Department of Biology, Arizona State University

Pebble Books

an imprint of Capstone Press
Mankato, Minnesota

Pebble Books are published by Capstone Press
151 Good Counsel Drive, P.O. Box 669, Mankato, Minnesota 56002
http://www.capstonepress.com

1 2 3 4 5 6 08 07 06 05 04 03

Library of Congress Cataloging-in-Publication Data
Trumbauer, Lisa, 1963–
    The life cycle of a cat/by Lisa Trumbauer.
    p. cm.—(Life cycles)
    Includes bibliographical references (p. 23) and index.
    Summary: Simple text and photographs present the life cycle of a cat.
    ISBN 0-7368-3391-9 (softcover) ISBN 0-7368-1182-6 (hardcover)
    1. Cats—Life cycles—Juvenile literature. [1. Cats. 2. Animals—Infancy.] I. Title
II. Life cycles (Mankato, Minn.)
SF445.7 .T78 2002
636.8—dc21
                                                               2001003108

Note to Parents and Teachers

The Life Cycles series supports national science standards related to life science. This book describes and illustrates the life cycle of a cat. The photographs support early readers in understanding the text. The repetition of words and phrases helps early readers learn new words. This book also introduces early readers to subject-specific vocabulary words, which are defined in the Words to Know section. Early readers may need assistance to read some words and to use the Table of Contents, Words to Know, Read More, Internet Sites, and Index/Word List sections of the book.

Table of Contents

Photographs in this book show the life cycle
of a tabby cat.

newborn

4

A cat begins life
as a kitten.

five days

6

Kittens are small when they are born. Their eyes are closed.
They cannot hear.

The mother cat takes care of her kittens. She carries them with her mouth.

ten days

Kittens grow quickly.
They can see and
hear after ten days.

two months

Kittens play and jump.

adult

14

A kitten becomes an adult after one year. A female cat attracts a male cat. The two cats mate.

Kittens begin to grow
inside the female's body.

The female cat gives birth after two months. She has a litter of kittens.

ten days

newborn

two months

adult

20

The kittens are the start of a new life cycle. Cats can live up to 20 years.

Words to Know

adult—an animal that is able to mate; some cats continue to grow larger after becoming adults.

attract—to get the attention of someone or something; when cats are attracted to each other, they move closer to each other.

life cycle—the stages in the life of an animal; the life cycle includes being born, growing up, having young, and dying.

litter—a group of animals born at the same time to one mother; cats usually have a litter of two to four kittens.

mate—to join together to produce young; cats can mate when they are about one year old.

Read More

Dolbear, Emily J., and E. Russell Primm. *Cats Have Kittens.* Animals and Their Young. Minneapolis: Compass Point Books, 2001.

Powell, Jillian. *From Kitten to Cat.* How Do They Grow? Austin, Texas: Raintree Steck-Vaughn, 2001.

Wallace, Holly. *Life Cycles.* Life Processes. Chicago: Heinemann Library, 2001.

Internet Sites

Cat Printout
http://www.enchantedlearning.com/subjects/mammals/cats/cat/catprintout.shtml

Fact Monster: Cat
http://klnlive.factmonster.com/ce6/sci/A0810811.html

Guide to Your Cat: The Life Stages
http://animal.discovery.com/cat_guide/lifestages.html

Index/Word List

Word Count: 108
Early-Intervention Level: 14

Editorial Credits

Sarah Lynn Schuette, editor; Jennifer Schonborn, production designer and interior illustrator; Kia Bielke, cover designer; Kimberly Danger and Mary Englar, photo researchers

Photo Credits

Behling and Johnson/Shirley Fernandez, 10, 18, 20 (top)
Dwight R. Kuhn, 4, 20 (left)
Norvia Behling, cover (bottom), 1, 6, 8, 12, 14, 16, 20 (right and bottom)
Visuals Unlimited/Gary Randall, cover (top)